DEDICATION

To my seven precious daughters. Each of you is a divine manifestation of God's guiding light, embodying the perfect and wondrous gifts that illuminate my path and embody the qualities I aspire for the world to witness.

Remember, life is a journey of unknowns, filled with strange and divine encounters, moments that will take surrender and selflessness, that will help you discover who you are meant to be. My greatest hope is that you embrace this adventure with creativity, love, and a relentless desire to serve God in all you do.

May you shine your light boldly in this world, chase your dreams with courage, and never forget that you were created with purpose.

ACKNOWLEDGEMENTS

Creating this book has been an incredible journey, and I am deeply grateful to those who have supported, inspired, and guided me along the way.

To my family—your love, encouragement, and belief in me have shaped my life and this book. To my children, who fill my world with creativity and wonder, you inspire me daily and remind me of the beauty in finding our place in the world as God intends. To my wife, who is more than a saint, your unwavering love and support mean more than words can express. To my parents, who have always loved me, challenged me to think deeply, and encouraged me to take on the impossible—thank you.

To Eljoh Hartzer, my editor—your insight and dedication have refined this book into something I am truly proud of.

To my father-in-law, David R. Shepherd—your guidance in structuring this book and navigating the publishing process has been invaluable. I could not have done this without your wisdom and support.

To Southwestern Assemblies of God University, thank you for providing a strong foundation of education and spiritual influence. The great teachers I learned from instilled in me the power of existential thought, shaping how I see the world of counseling and engage with ideas.

To Margaret Owens, your incredible illustrations have breathed life into these pages, turning words into something truly magical. Thank you for sharing your artistry and vision.

And above all, to God—for saving me, teaching me, and walking this journey out with me. Every step, every word, and every lesson has been because of You.

THE COSMIC ADVENTURES OF ZARA AND FRIENDS

A Tale of Identity

Author
JONATHAN A. BOYE

Illustrator
MARGARET OWENS

A Resource of Arcadian Therapeutic Services

ARCADIAN
THERAPEUTIC SERVICES

The Cosmic Adventures of Zara and Friends: A Tale of Identity
Copyright © 2025 by Jonathan A. Boye
All rights reserved

Illustrations by Margaret Owens
Spring Hill, Tennessee
https://www.facebook.com/p/Margaret-Owens-Art-100093252590240

Cover and interior design by Lauren Murrell Graphic Design
Hendersonville, Tennessee
murrell.lauren@gmail.com

All Scripture quotations are from The Passion Translation®.
Copyright © 2017, 2018, 2020 by Passion & Fire Ministries, Inc.
Used by permission. All rights reserved.
ThePassionTranslation.com.

Published in association with the DRS Agency

Franklin, Tennessee
drsagency.com

Printed in the USA

MESSAGE FROM THE AUTHOR

In this book, you'll meet Zara, a unique star designed by Divinus Nebula who travels through the cosmos. Along the way, she discovers her purpose and the friends who will stand by her side. I intend to tell a story to help readers process aspects of identity connection and help with the stirring question of existence. The message is powerful and aims to combine ideas from theology, philosophy, and psychology (counseling).

Reflection questions are located in the last section of the book.

Readers can either complete the story before moving into reflection or visit the questions at the end of each chapter. This latter method is suggested for groups journeying through the book together.

After meeting Zara and her friends, I hope readers will explore aspects of their true identity and Creator. Enjoy the journey!

*Rise up in splendor and be radiant,
for your light has dawned,
and Yahweh's glory now streams from you!
Look carefully!
Darkness blankets the earth,
and thick gloom covers the nations,
but Yahweh arises upon you
and the brightness of his glory
appears over you!*

ISAIAH 60:1-3 TPT

CHAPTER 1
The Lonely Star

Nestled in the far reaches of the great expanse above, a vel of shimmering lights prepared to celebrate an extraordinary event. In the darkness of space, something incredible was about to happen...

A new star with a future yet to be written was about to be born. The astronomical being's inception would begin in a place filled with angelic gasses and etheric winds in what is called a nebula, a star's nursery. The birthing place of this star was known as Divinus. On this particular day, Divinus's mystical breath blew on the glistening gasses, causing them to arch and spin in a symphony of stardust to create a star

unlike any other. Out of the churning, this star would be known as Zara, meaning *radiant*, as her heart would become.

Fragments of stardust combined with Devinus's fertility; the universe welcomed her and celebrated this new life. With this latest creation, the eternal held His breath, eager to witness the unfolding of her divine value. The sacred intent behind this birth was clear: she was made to shine, to be a glimmer of hope in the vast emptiness of space.

Yet, beneath the shining facade, Zara was already aware of an uncomfortable yearning; angst was swiftly growing in her awakening thoughts.

As she took her first breath, she found herself contemplating identity, the purpose of her being, and pondering the ontological knowing that would create meaning for her cravings:

Who am I?
Why am I here?
Why do I shine?
What am I made of?
How do I fit into the greater universe?

CHAPTER 2
Embarking on the Unknown

Amid the dark matter of the expanse of space, a spark ignited within Zara's being, setting her aflame with determination and a deep desire to define her reason for existence. She could hear the whispers of curiosities growing, which led her to want to address her longing wonderment; she conceived a courageous idea...

She fantasized about a path to answer her questions, charting a new course where no star had gone before. She dreamed of finding someone who could satisfy this craving. She felt the only way to answer this was to step out in faith and travel to the unknown. Little did she know that this journey would be a quest for belonging and self-exploration, leaving a lasting legacy.

Zara found the courage to shape her map, infusing it with her hopes and the humility she learned from watching Divinus. The route took shape—a delicate masterpiece of curves and light, echoing the vast beauty of the celestial surroundings.

Through her diligence in research, Zara's path became crystal clear: a remote galaxy named Stella 9. Rumors had been circulating that galaxies in other reaches of the universe had helped other longing souls find a place of peace, where one could see clearly and where questions found their answers.

Zara gazed down at the route she had mapped out and hesitated momentarily before taking the first step of faith and bidding farewell to her place of birth, familiarity, love, and safety. Her heart's curiosity fueled the spark for her trajectory, leaving behind a delicate trail of stardust.

With an anticipatory heart and silent voice in her head, Zara's mind whispered into the chasm of space:

"Guide me. Lead me. Please answer my inner yearning."

CHAPTER 3
A Radiant Bond

It was not long before Zara realized that a patient heart would be needed for this journey. It was not a direct path, and she regularly wandered off the planned route.

Her first stop caused her to cross paths with a comet named Claudius. This comet was a universal wanderer born of the distant Oort Cloud, a region teeming with frozen remnants from his solar system's early days. An age-old aura of wisdom radiating from him had a magnetic pull on Zara.

Zara was fascinated by Claudius's story. Surely, he must have asked these same questions on his circular journeys and, perhaps, even gotten some answers. *Perhaps this confident comet might help me discover the answers I so desperately seek, too,* she thought.

Zara's light took Claudius to a place of awe. She seemed completely unaware of her brilliance's effect on her surroundings. The stardust rhythm evoked a sense of grace, passion, and beauty around her every move as she pioneered her path through the dark abyss of space—a light shining in the darkness.

In Claudius, Zara found a kindred spirit—a fellow traveler who was also on a journey of self-discovery.

Zara whispered, *"Do you know who you are or why you were put into existence? Has your journey answered your calling of existence?"*

Claudius responded with a simple yet profound declaration, *"I've circled the far reaches of creation that others only dream about. Those experiences came with stories and shared experiences of the expanse of space that answered some of my questions - and may answer yours too."*

Hearing this, she gained a certain confidence, which caused Zara's mind to whirl with thoughts. *"How do you define yourself?"* she bravely asked.

Claudius responded peacefully: *"I am a comet designed by the Creator as a kind of snowball with a dazzling tale, as a crusader through space, imparting wisdom to those I come in contact with."*

Zara thought for a minute, then replied, *"I don't look like a comet, but should I act like one or even become you? Is that why the Creator made me?"*

With gentleness, Claudius replied, "No, young one. But since we all are part of a grander plan, you will forever share in the tapestry of my journey. Yet, just as I am a fragment of the Creator's story, you are an irreplaceable thread woven into the grand design. You will find your place soon enough."

Moved by this connection, Zara felt a mixture of emotions. For a fleeting moment, she sensed an amicable attachment, a beautiful belonging, a universal union. Yet, she knew from deep within that her quest was not over.

She felt pulled between continuing her journey and staying with Claudius to hear about his adventures. A wanting within her to experience the warmth of friendship she had never felt before to address a feeling of loneliness; recognizing that the darkness and fear of the journey were bringing in her loneliness. She chose to step out and boldly invited him to join her on a new adventure. Claudius's response mirrored his embrace of life's mysteries: "I have longed to feel the gravitational pull of a star *and to share my wisdom with a willing soul.*"

Zara and Claudius set forth toward Stella 9. Her spirit was unyielding, and her desire for revelation burned ever brighter. This time, with her new friend by her side, she would not be alone in her passion for answers against the backdrop of creation's mysteries.

CHAPTER 4
SPREADING LIGHT TO THE VOID

As Zara and Claudius advanced, they saw that the route was like a river they could navigate but never control. As unexpected currents pulled them along, Claudius taught Zara that she had a choice in responding. He also shared that he had learned that unraveling the essence of one's ontological experience involves mindful curiosity.

Wherever Zara went, light followed. Unknowingly, her brilliance ignited a revolution. Zara illuminated the once-veiled darkness, revealing a previously unnoticed cluster of four planets. Zara's light reached the icy realms that the Exo Siblings called home. These Planetary siblings had hovered in isolation for a long time.

Now, they basked in a warmth they had never experienced before. Zara's glowing light had opened their eyes to their hidden polychromatic palette – for multicolored did not quite describe their beauty. They were amazed to see their orbits, designed in geometric waves. Their collective presence was seen as an enchantment of irradiated hues like a kaleidoscope revealing a purpose transcending individuality – a purpose they could only glimpse thanks to Zara's presence.

As Zara and Claudius journeyed towards them, they and the Exo Siblings formed a fantastic connection. Zara's voice carried existential questions, sparking contemplation and self-discovery among the four Exo siblings: Vega, Nesus, Orionis, and Lyra.

"Have you ever pondered the significance of identity in a seemingly disconnected creation? It might all seem random, but there is more to us than meets the eye. We share a purpose, a mission, and a reason for being. I want to find out what that is..." As Zara's words resonated through the atmosphere, the comet Claudius circled Zara, nodding in agreement.

The Exo siblings responded one by one:

Vega's gentle shimmer held a hint of wonderment: *"As we stand united in this glowing understanding, I wonder if seeing ourselves in your light is shedding light on that true purpose?"*

Nesus reacted next: *"We have always had an identity! But until the value of our creation was realized by light, we were masked and could not find that meaning."*

Orionis responded with intrigue: *"Indeed, the light you bring to our darkness reflects a deeper truth about who we are and who we were created to be, now that we can see."*

Lyra reacted: *"And Claudius, I see how your wisdom truly guides Zara as she explores these questions she seeks. You are speaking into her journey, teaching her about how others and you have found answers to ponderings, which I know will help us all."*

So, each of the Exo Siblings declared their newfound light on their identity, which would have been impossible without the illumination of another. Standing at Zara's side in his shimmering form, Claudius resonated with quiet joy: *"Just as I've walked the paths of the universe, so we shall all continue walking, binding in mutuality."*

Zara's heart exploded with joy and a growing belonging she could not yet describe. The path ahead remained unknown. Nevertheless, they would traverse it together—a group with a shared hunger to understand their place in creation and why they felt their journey was not one of randomness. For Zara, she felt a kinship that she could not explain, and it left her with more questions.

CHAPTER 5
The Shadowed Encounter

As the group of friends journeyed through the cosmos, following Zara's charted course toward Stella 9, the path was all but predictable. Most of their experiences brimming with the duality of emotions—they glided along the galaxy effortlessly. But one day, that all changed.

Because Zara was leading the way, she felt the pull of a dark presence. She held her breath and gazed into a sonicating abyss. Claudius said, *"Be careful, for*

I have seen this before. Other astral bodies have called this a black hole because what falls in can't escape."

Zara's curiosity found themselves at the rim of a black hole named Gravus. Zara and her friends could not help but notice the subtle dimming of their radiance as they approached him. The intense gravitational pull made them abandon their path.

Gravus taunted her passion for purpose: *"Identity? Purpose? What does it matter? Creation is a vast expanse of chaos and isolation. We're all just wandering... searching for meaning that doesn't exist."*

Claudius and the Exo Siblings looked nervous as Zara took a step forward. She looked at Gravus with empathy, her passion unquenched. *"But isn't the wandering, the shared journey, itself a form of connection?"* she asked.

"Everything in life will disappear, and I will be alone no matter what. Meaningless! Utterly meaningless!" Gravus sighed. As he spoke, his gravitational pull intensified.

The comet Claudius and the Exo Siblings knew that Zara would keep probing further, so they linked arms to pull Zara back should she go over the edge. But Zara was driven by her commitment to curiosity, commensurability, and compassion, so she empathetically questioned Gravus further: *"Look how you're pulling me in now - doesn't your absorbing presence impact the constructs around you and prove that you have a value hinting at purpose?"*

Gravus revealed a vulnerable gaze as he contemplated what she was suggesting: the potential for hearts to radiate even in the darkest depths. He was finally about to see past the darkness that had clouded his vision for so long, and that was when he saw that Zara was fading and growing dim. She looked at him with bravery in her eyes, willing to give part of her light to him despite his track record of extinguishing light. He also looked beyond her and noticed for the first time the friends who had linked up with their gravitational pull of love were waiting to save Zara if needed.

Gravus looked up to see this bond and willingness of love that had never been present in his life before. Tears began to appear in his eyes, and he slowly nodded to welcome Zara's embrace. Gradually, Gravus shed his darkness, embracing a newfound radiance, and the friends saw that he was pretty beautiful, bathed in forgiving light.

CHAPTER 6
THE GREAT ALTAR OF TOMORROW

$\mathcal{E}$ach group's experiences painted a vibrant narrative upon the infinite space canvas. After the encounter with the black hole, it took them a while to find their path again. The comet Claudius used his age-old wisdom of the galaxy to guide them back to their route. They could see Stella 9 in the distance and looked at each other with hope as they journeyed forward. Suddenly, as if out of nowhere, they saw a bright light shoot across the sky and stood still in awe.

They were witnessing the intense surge of a supernova - a star dying. As they approached the supernova, sadness and fear enveloped them. The light kept getting brighter and brighter until they had to look away because its brilliance was too much.

Claudius, the comet that had traversed the expanse of space for so many years, comprehended the silent language of stars and nodded in recognition and acceptance of profound grief. But Zara and the Exo Siblings were in tears. They exclaimed with worry when they saw that the supernova was taking her planets down with her.

As they approached, they saw the planets' willingness to die with the star that had fed them and provided them with an orbit.

Zara looked into the brilliant light and said, *"Dear supernova, why do you offer yourself to the cosmos? And why would your other celestial bodies be willing to lay down their lives with yours?"*

The supernova's light pulsed, acknowledging Zara's words. Then came the answer: *"I enjoyed giving of myself to these planets. Transcendence was a priceless gift so others may ascend to greater heights than I ever did. I hope their achievements are better than my own."*

Claudius added his voice to the conversation: *"In your sacrifice, you are not lost but transformed. Your light lives on within the creation, inspiring and nurturing other stars that follow your path, leaving behind a legacy."* Then he turned to the Exo Siblings and whispered, *"Did you know that light can never be destroyed? It lives on forever but takes different forms. She is dying, but her light will live on. FHersacrifice will become the testament that the main stars will be born again in many more stars' lives. For one life given will be the heart of millions to have a life!"*

As they stood in the presence of this radiant sacrifice, the collective radiance of the group of friends seemed to intermingle with the supernova's fading glow. They realized that just as the dying star's light would continue to influence the universe for generations to come, their shared journey also had the potential to impact the cosmos around them if they could live the same fearless and self-sacrificing existence.

CHAPTER 7
Embrace of Stella 9

*I*n the infinite expanse of the cosmos, Zara and her companions embarked on the final leg of their journey toward the heart of the distant galaxy named Stella 9. Zara felt a tug at her heart, an irresistible connection drawing her to embrace the peace here in Stella 9. The Exo Siblings shared in this sensation, their radiant presence intensifying as they neared their destination. Claudius flew with his quiet confidence into this long-awaited place of peace.

With glistening eyes and minds full of questions, they took their final steps toward their destination. As they arrived in the embrace of Stella 9's aura, a remarkable transformation occurred...

The framework of the Heavens seemed to move and gleam in response to these sojourners' merging. It was as if their arrival had been awaited for quite some time. A welcoming echoed through the boundless currents of her being. Zara sensed a gentle murmuring from within and spoke in words and emotions, which helped them grow their understanding.

"Welcome, dear travelers! You are not mere sojourners but integral, entwined realities in the grand plan of Divinus."

Zara pondered, *But why did he not speak this from the beginning?*

"Your journey mirrors the divine dance of creation itself - from birth to wanting emotions, to acceptances that lead one's curiosity, vulnerability, awareness, and connection - which leads all to find the heart of their transcendence in existence. From birth, you were bound by the intention of existence to face critical questions: What was the intention of the Creator to place me in this universe, and what value do I have to offer it?"

Zara said, *"Yes, what is my value in this Universe?"*

"You have been searching for answers in the desert of space; you encountered wise sojourners to listen to, walk with, and share everyday experiences. You were not meant to be alone in your attempts to subdue your offerings from the Creator. He delights in your freedom to interact with his artistry with freedom even though it sometimes comes at a cost."

Zara's heart swelled. The voice implied that creation was not a random collection of isolated entities but a web of interwoven stories and shared experiences. It was a narrative that celebrated identity, growth, and the boundless potential of connection - bringing light to one's purpose.

With a sense of awe, Zara and her companions stood in the peaceful embrace of Stella 9, basking in the shared wisdom that surrounded them. Here in Stella 9, they had complete clarity about identity, purpose, and meaning in creation.

Thus, beneath the canopy, the harmony of heavenly bodies continued to compose its melodious opus. It was a melody that celebrated the odyssey of life, the profound influence of connection, and the enduring brilliance of the Creator's majestic design.

Here, Zara grasped her ontologically designed true self:

"I am a star that exists to be a celestial body that will undergo various stages of life, with many experiences that will shape my journey with other interconnected bodies. The reaction of nuclear fusion makes me up, giving off heat and light to my companions so they may live out their potential. This is all done according to the design of the Divine value the Creator has given all of us. I am born, will change, grow in wisdom, and accept my potential fate, which means I will live my best life in the given time. This will be done by embracing those who teach me and walk alongside me, those who steward the comprehension of their ontological value. The Creator gave me these things so that I might also give to others."

She exhaled contently as she looked around at the friends she made along the journey.

She whispered a soft *"Thank you,"* hoping the Creator of it all heard her.

Reflection Questions

CHAPTER 1: THE LONELY STAR

Keywords

Purpose, meaning, identity, place, isolation, curiosity

Questions

- What does it mean to have an ontological understanding?
- Why is defining identity, purpose, and meaning essential?
- **Angst** is a term often used to describe *existential anxiety or dread, reflecting the apprehension one may feel when confronting the inherent uncertainties of existence.*
  Do you identify with the angst Zara felt? Why or why not?
- What is the significance of identity in a seemingly disconnected creation?
- What is the purpose of existence, and how does one find their place in the cosmos?
- How do feelings of isolation and curiosity shape one's quest for meaning?
- What was Zara's purpose?
- What does Zara's name mean about who she was made and how she lived this out at the end of the story?

CHAPTER 2: EMBARKING ON THE UNKNOWN

Keywords

core desire, destination, belonging, inner yearning

Questions

- Do we have the freedom to construct our path and destiny in the vast expanse of existence? Is our life a blank slate to write our understanding of existence?

- What core desires and questions can you identify that all people share?

- Define what is meant by "reason for being."

- Do we need to build something (like Zara's map) that can help us understand our destination?

- What is the significance of the parallel between Zara's story and our quest for meaning?

- Stella 9 "was known to be a place of peace where one could see clearly and where questions found their answers." What emotion does it bring to you to think about such a place?

- What does it mean to you to belong?

- **Ephemeral** can signify *the transient and fleeting nature of life, experiences, and moments*. How is this seen in the story so far?

CHAPTER 3: A RADIANT BOND

Keywords

Wisdom, kindred spirit, grander plan, Creator, connection

Questions

- How does connection with others impact one's journey of self-discovery positively? And negatively?
- What do you think about when Zara feels an "amicable attachment, a beautiful belonging, a universal union"? Can you think of a moment when you had a similar feeling?
- A **temporal perspective** can be defined as *emphasizing the importance of considering past, present, and future experiences in understanding one's existence.* Where do you see this kind of perspective in this chapter?
- What draws Zara to Claudius? And what draws Claudius to Zara?
- How can kindred spirits and mentors shape one's path and understanding of existence?
- Who is on the journey with you?
- Notice the questions that Zara asks Claudius and how he responds. Write down three questions you have and think of someone you can ask.
- Why did Claudius choose to accompany Zara on the journey if he knew the answers?

CHAPTER 4:
SPREADING LIGHT TO THE SHY

Keywords

brilliance, isolation, darkness, united, true purpose, wisdom

Questions

- The journey is described as a river they could navigate but never control. What does this say about life?

- Why did the Exo Siblings need Zara?

- What is the significance of recognizing the potential within us and others?

- How do others (mentors and kindred spirits) play a part in discovering who we are?

- Who are people in your life to whom you need to give of yourself and help them see the truth of their existence?

- In *Bibliotherapy*, the belief is that sharing stories can have a profound healing effect. How is this seen in the group of friends?

- What do you think about when you hear the word 'polychromatic'? What are three other words that you can think of to describe God's creation and fully grasp one's true design and purpose in this universe? There is a balance between two Latin words, 'a priori' (reasoning) and 'a posteriori' (experiential learning). How do you see these play out in this chapter?

CHAPTER 5: THE SHADOWED ENCOUNTER

Keywords

unpredictable, meaning, fading, shedding darkness

Questions

* How does embracing one's unique frailty and pain within one's story contribute to a sense of purpose?

* Are there lies within your life currently distracting you from your journey?

* How does the nature of darkness and negativity in cosmic space affect one's perception of meaning and connection?

* Can individuals consumed by darkness find solace and transformation through connection and acceptance?

* How does the power of friendship and empathy bridge the gap between light and darkness?

* Look at this definition of **commensurability** -
  Finding common ground or shared meaning in communication and understanding between individuals is challenging.
  How do you see this play out in the chapter?

* What would have happened if Zara's friends had not been with her when she encountered Gravus?

* What changes in Gravus from the beginning to the end of this chapter? How did that transformation occur?

CHAPTER 6:
THE GREAT ALTAR OF TOMORROW

Keywords

Hope, sadness, selflessness, transcendence, legacy

Questions

- How does sacrifice, like that of the supernova, contribute to the greater sacrificial narrative?

- Is the goal of life to arrive at one's transcendence? What does that mean?

- Can you think of a person or two who you know that have arrived at transcendence? How can you learn from them?

- How do Zara's thoughts echo the age-old story of a different kind of sacrifice— that of Jesus Christ?

- A well-worn path of sacrifice and selflessness always leaves behind a legacy, even though that is never the intent. What legacy are you leaving behind?

- Think of the legacy left behind by the apostles, Mother Teresa or Martin Luther. What do they have in common?

- What do you think about the fact that light can never be destroyed? What does that say about our spiritual journeys?

CHAPTER 7: EMBRACE OF STELLA 9

Keywords

connection, destination, transformation, whisper

Questions

- How does the cosmic journey mirror life's journey, from birth to curiosity to vulnerability to awareness?
- What was the significance of shared experiences and connections in the grand tapestry of existence?
- What story do you want to write for yourself so that you will feel that you have finished the journey well at the end of your life?
- Imagine arriving at your true identity, purpose, and meaning. What would you feel?
- What does the word 'interconnectedness' bring to mind? Do you feel connected or isolated?
- What are the answers to Zara's questions from Chapter 1? *(Who am I? Why am I here? What is my purpose?)*
- The whisper mentions a fundamental question: *"How shall I live and impact the world?"* Take time now to reflect on this question as you consider the journey described in this story.

OVERALL REFLECTION
ON THE STORY AS A WHOLE

Definitions and exploration of awareness (This will take some time to explore and understand outside of the book.)

A Priori Knowledge

Knowledge is derived from reason, deduction, or innate concepts. Logical propositions and certain metaphysical principles are often considered a *priori* knowledge. Studying a *priori* knowledge involves examining abstract concepts and reasoning independently of specific doing.

Take a moment and look at the story and your own life to determine and become aware of what in one's life is *priori* understanding:

1. Identity: We understand that our priori awareness of identity is that we are an independent creation and can not be anything else.

2. The Concept of Necessity: Our existence is not unplanned but uniquely intentional. In your ontological being, you can feel a profound, reflexive understanding that you exist, even if you're unsure how your existence manifests over time.

Now your turn

3. Time and Change:

4. The Nature of Possibility and Potential:

5. Sense of Autonomy:

6. Ethical Responsibility and Moral Agency:

7. Intuition of Willingness:

A Posteriori Knowledge

Posteriori knowledge is based on empirical observations and experiences. Scientific observations, historical facts, and sensory perceptions fall into this category. Studying a *posteriori* knowledge involves engaging with the concrete world and drawing conclusions from observable phenomena.

1. For Identity: When we look back on our lives, we can see the divine footprint of our creation.
2. For Necessity: The events, relationships, and challenges the divine have walked out of our purpose.

Now your turn

3. Time and Change:

4. The Nature of Possibility and Potential:

5. Sense of Autonomy:

6. Ethical Responsibility and Moral Agency:

7. Intuition of Willingness:

Dasein

Dasein is a term associated with existential philosophy, particularly Martin Heidegger's works. It refers to the unique mode of being or existence that humans possess. *Dasein* implies an awareness of one's existence and the ability to engage with the world.

1. What is your experience with this moment here and now?
2. How do I understand my place and interaction with the present world?
3. What is it like to exist in the world?
4. How does my awareness of morality and ethics shape my life?
5. What does it mean for me to walk in "authenticity" now?
6. How do I engage with the future?
7. What does it mean to live with and be with others?

Questions

- How did this story of Zara and her friends help you better understand each of these concepts defined above?
- Both a priori and posteriori knowledge must be applied to understand existence fully. Why is this true?
- How do you understand Dasein after reading this story?
- A few themes run like a golden thread through this story; can you identify a few?
- Example: light versus darkness
- Use the following table to summarize how you interpreted the characters/events in this story and how they relate to your own life.

ZARA	*Example:* I see myself as Zara. I identify with her questions and her search for purpose and belonging.
ZARA	
THE MAP	
CLAUDIUS THE COMET	
EXO SIBLINGS	

Gravus, the black hole
(Chapter 5)

The Supernova
(Chapter 6)

Stella 9

Creator

www.ingramcontent.com/pod-product-compliance
Lightning Source LLC
Chambersburg PA
CBHW041521070526
44585CB00002B/29